LOVE T.A.P.S.

Red Flags of An Abuser & How to Get Out

Candyce "Ce" Anderson, M.S., L.P.C.

The contents herein are for informational and educational purposes only, not legal advice, based on the author's research and experience as a licensed clinical mental health therapist. Please consult your doctor or mental health professional regarding the best course of treatment for you.

Cover design by
Stacey Bowers, August Pride, Inc.
www.augustpride.com
Tusks & Whiskers Design, Co.
Editing by EA Writing Services

Copyright © 2016 by Ce Consulting, LLC
All rights reserved. This book or any portion thereof may not be reproduced or used in any manner whatsoever without the express written permission of the publisher except for the use of brief quotations in a book review.

Printed in the United States of America

First Printing, 2016

ISBN-13: 978-1539785552

ISBN-10: 1539785556

Ce Consulting, LLC
PO Box 230938
Montgomery, AL 36123
www.lovetapsbook.com

Dedications

This book is dedicated to my angels along the way:

My amazing husband & beautiful family
My Howard University & Elite 13 sisters
Frazer O., Erica B. & Shirley M.
Mishondy & Candice
The Family Sunshine Center
W.E.A.V.

Preface

There are a myriad of circumstances that could have led to you being in this relationship. Perhaps you were abused as a child, or you have unmet emotional needs. Maybe you have it all together; the dream career, money in the bank, a beautiful home and fate simply landed you here. Regardless of how you ended up in this toxic relationship, you do not have to stay. There is hope.

In this book, you will find explicit, evidence-based examples that will help you decipher whether your relationship is abusive or not and if so, how to make a safe exit. <u>Anyone</u> can be a victim; men, women, black, white, rich, poor, gay, or straight. Intimate partner violence does not discriminate. With that, this book will cover specifically intimate partner violence, which is violence between two individuals who are or have been sexually and or romantically involved, although domestic violence can exist between siblings, parents and children, and roommates. For the purposes of this book, I will, at times, refer to the victim and the abuser using feminine and masculine pronouns respectively, as statistics show that 90% of victims are female and their abusers are males.

However, please substitute the appropriate pronouns that describe your gender identity and that of your significant other.

Most abusers are strategic, highly intelligent, and predatory. Their ability to observe and select their victim is uncanny. This takes time, diligence, and charisma. It is not by happenstance that this person selected you as their target; again, this is strategic. To save your well-being, sanity, children, and life, you too must be strategic and informed. And remember, **it is not your fault.** I pray that this book is one of many resources you find to exit and abusive relationship safely and live the life that you deserve. You are valuable and this world needs you.

Contents

1. It's Not Domestic Violence If I Don't Get Hit
2. Two Types of Victims; Two Types of Abusers
3. The Charmer; the Good Times
4. The Ex Factor
5. Falling in Love; the Whirlwind Romance
6. Isolation: I want you all to myself
7. Gas Lighting
8. Green Eyes & Eggshells
9. Deception: Lies, Omissions & Trickery
10. Pity Party for One
11. Submission: What does God say?
12. Abuse Trauma & Your Children
13. Your Relationship in Review
14. Barriers to Leaving
15. Making Your Exit
16. Healing and Healthy Dating
17. Questions & Answers
18. Statistics & Resources

About The Author

Suggested Reading

Chapter 1

"The scars from mental cruelty can be as deep and long-lasting as wounds from punches or slaps but are often not as obvious..." – Lundy Bancroft

It's Not Domestic Violence If I Don't Get Hit

In practice, I have come across many victims both male and female, who believe society's view of domestic violence – the physical abuse. We have learned to associate "wife-beater" tank tops, beer cans, and unemployed, aggressive men with violence against women. Abuse comes in many forms, just as its victims. What if I told you that physical abuse is not at the core of abuse, but that power and control are the real culprits?

The U.S. Department of Justice (2015) defines domestic violence as follows: "a pattern of abusive behavior in any relationship that is used by one partner to gain or maintain power and control over another intimate partner". Therefor the motivation behind the actual abuse is power and control.

To gain this power and control over the other person, the perpetrator may use tactics that manifest as abuse that is physical, emotional, psychological, sexual, or even financial. Let's unpack each of these manifestations.

Physical Abuse - This type of abuse is overtly displayed through use of bodily harm, and intimidation. This can include hitting, slapping, poking, punching, scratching, kicking, pushing, shoving, choking, pinching, spitting, and use of objects or weapons to cause bodily harm.

Sexual Abuse - Sexual abuse not only includes rape but also molestation, coercive sexual contact, and demanding sex. The victim may be asleep or incapacitated, and the abuser then engages in sexual contact without permission. This is sexual assault, even if the victim and abuser are married. If you do not give permission, it is assault. Period.

Psychological Abuse - This is the abuse of one's mind, thoughts, and will. This includes making light of serious issues that affect the person, making light of abusive behavior, shifting the responsibility of the abuse onto the victim, jealousy and isolation, as well as restricting one's ability to move about freely.

Emotional Abuse - As with the other forms of abuse, emotional abuse can be devastating, particularly for a victim who has suffered previous or childhood traumas. This includes being subjected to putdowns, emotionally degraded, teased, name calling, guilt tripping, withholding affection, gas lighting and the silent treatment. The perpetrator literally causes the victim to second-guess their sanity and mental wellness.

Financial Abuse - This includes restricting the victim's access to money and means of financial independence. This is accomplished by withholding account information or forbidding the victim from working, using or withdrawing money. Financial abuse also includes requiring the victim to account for his or her income, or being giving an allowance. Whether the income is earned or dispersed to the victim as state-based or government assistance/benefits, the withholding of this from one by another is also financial abuse. Perpetrators sometimes even force their victims to solicit money from family members, community resource agencies, or steal from his or her place of employment.

Here are several abuse tactics that can be cross-categorized:

Intimidation. Destruction of the victim's property including treasured items, work necessities, or a vehicle. Intimidation can also take the form of the use physical abuse using gestures or intimating looks in order to manipulate the victim, as well as "bucking" and punching walls.

Coercion. Perpetrators will sometimes threaten to leave their partner or commit suicide to prevent the end of the relationship. Victims may be coerced or threatened into committing illegal activities. Sexual coercion is also common. Many women have been coerced into performing sexual acts with their abuser's friends.

Use of Male Privilege. This form of abuse includes the perpetrator having a regimented schedule that the victim is expected to follow, including the preparation of dinner, sex, cleaning, etc. This may also entail using "male privilege" to degrade the female, making her feel less-than because she is a woman, in which case, he is the "king" of the house and you are the servant. Despite what we see in movies and on television, intimate partner violence does not have to be physical to hurt, harm or damage you.

Chapter 2

Two Types of Victims; Two Types of Abusers

In cases where power and control exists, you will find that an abuser usually fits into one of two categories: emotionally wounded or pathologically disturbed. According to Cleckley (1964), perpetrators that are emotionally damaged or wounded can manifest themselves as a mama's boy, a jerk, or through refusing to commit. This individual may have witnessed violence as a child and learned to take on the role of an abuser. He may show disregard for his partner's feelings, be physically abusive, or emotionally unavailable, among other things. Through individual therapy, if he chooses, he can process the emotional trauma that contributed to his pathology as an abuser.

The pathologically disturbed abuser or antisocial personality disorder abuser is quite different in that both his environment and childhood experiences, (i.e. severe abuse or neglect along with the genetic predisposition to mental illness), have contributed to the disorder. This is known as a diathesis. This person is not concerned with consequences of his actions and in his twisted and damaged mind, the laws that apply to the average citizen do not apply to him.

The difference between these two types is that the emotionally wounded abuser does not seek to harm the partner when he or she ends the relationship. In contrast, the sociopathic abuser becomes dangerous, seeking to harm the partner. Sandra Brown describes this individual as having no ability to: (1) sustain positive change, (2) develop to a place emotional or spiritual depth and (3) cultivate insight about their effect on others. In essence, she describes the hallmarks of a sociopathic abuser.

I cannot stress enough the dangers of an individual with anti-social personality disorder. Although it is unethical to diagnose a person without formal assessment by a licensed clinician, for educational purposes only, I will list the characteristics of this disorder according to the Diagnostic & Statistical Manual for Mental Disorders V (DSM-5):

- Failure to conform to social norms (i.e lawful behaviors or following rules)

- Deceitfulness, as indicated by repeated lying, use of aliases, and conning others
- Impulsivity or failure to plan ahead
- Irritability and aggressiveness as indicated by repeated fights/assaults
- Reckless disregard for safety of self and others
- Consistent irresponsibility, as indicated by repeated failure to sustain consistent work behavior or honor financial obligations
- Lack of remorse, as indicated by being indifferent to or rationalizing having hurt, mistreated, or stolen from another

Note that traits may not be visible in the beginning, as he or she will go to great lengths to mask their true self. If you are patient, however, and mindful of what you learn in this book, you will be able to recognize the very subtle cues of this type of abuser.

Chapter 3

CHARM /CHärm/
noun

1. *the power or quality of giving delight or arousing admiration.*

verb

1. *delight greatly; allure, fascinate*
2. *control or achieve by or as if by magic.*

The Charmer; the Good Times

In the beginning, Lana and Maurice seemed like the perfect couple. Maurice was attentive and loving. He showered Lana with attention, took care of small projects around her house without asking, and always greeting her with some token of affection, be it flowers, a lovely note, or her favorite candy. Unlike a previous relationship, Maurice had even invited Lana to a family gathering to introduce her as his girlfriend. She had finally found the man she longed for, and in fact, she prayed for his arrival in her life. He walked, talked, and acted just like she had hoped. But that is just it, he was acting.

Love bombing is a process where the abuser strategically becomes all that the unsuspecting partner desires. It is during this phase of the relationship that our brains release oxytocin and dopamine especially during sexual encounters. Everything literally feels great. Later in the relationship, at the onset of abuse whether physical or otherwise, the victim will either remember or be reminded by the abuser of how it "used" to be. The good times. The abused partner may see an abusive incident as isolated or the result of some extenuating circumstance such as stress, anger, or alcohol. The victim may say things like:

"I remember how it used to be…"

"She wasn't like this in the beginning."

"It will get better if we could just…"

"He's not a bad person."

This often leads to the abused partner believing that if they could just get back to how it was, they can reclaim that loving feeling. How would Lana accomplish this fleeting task? Perhaps couples counseling. A few sessions and things will be as they once were. Not so fast.

In the domestic violence prevention community, there is a standard: couples counseling in NOT recommended in a relationship where domestic violence has taken place for several reasons. I will list a few:

- Couples counseling hinges on both partners in the relationship taking responsibility. The only responsible partner in an abusive relationship is the abuser.
- Remember what is at the core of an abusive relationship: power and control. Can you be authentic when you're being controlled or manipulated, or when your thoughts and feelings are being invalidated? Would that therapy session be a safe place to disclose? Probably not.
- Often the victim believes, and is told, that the relationship's issues are solely their fault. The abuser believes it also. So then, why would he need to go to counseling?
- Many counselors do not have knowledge or experience with domestic violence dynamics. There's probably a chapter in a textbook or materials from a workshop that gave them a few tips but it takes a skilled clinician to recognize the nuances of such circumstances.

Here's an example. Let's say that in a counseling session, Lana reveals that Maurice physically intimidates her on a regular basis. She explains that he never hit her, but that he got in her face, stared intensely, and that his upper body swelled. Maurice vehemently denies this blaming it on her "imagination" while the counselor glosses over it. This may seem small, but the counselor simply has unknowingly formed an alliance in the mind of the abuser, reinforcing Maurice's ability to control and take power. Can't you just hear him during the couple's next argument, "See, just like the therapist said, you are always imagining things! Nobody's abusing you!"

If you are hoping that couples' counseling will fix your relationship, please think it over. I would suggest that you concentrate on your *own* mental health and wellness and not that of the partner. You cannot, nor can a therapist, change someone that does not recognize they have a problem.

Chapter 4

The Ex Factor

Courtney was a smooth guy. Charismatic, a blue collar worker, and seemed loving at first glance. One could say that he adored Lisa. Lisa wasn't overly concerned about Courtney's past, but when she would ask about his previous relationships, he either refused to answer her questions or he would refer to his ex-girlfriends as "crazy". Have you heard this before? "My ex was crazy! She used to go through my phone, call the numbers of female contacts, and check my social media. She even had my bank account information." You may have even heard "my ex won't stay away from my family; she even tries to be close with my mother."

What an abuser probably won't say is that, he may have cheated, sent her on an emotional roller-coaster, played psychological and emotional games with her, and led her on. No. She is just a stalker for no reason. Granted, some people have a difficult time letting go, but folks that hang on usually do so because the other person, your new boo in this case, continues to give her hope. This is a sign ladies and gentlemen. Here is why: in a healthy relationship, it takes two to make or break the relationship. That means that both parties are somewhat responsible for the break-up. If your partner is blaming his ex *and* vilifying the person, pay close attention. Now there are cases where someone has truly been with a disturbed partner and they have truly fled the relationship for safety. However, there are more instances where the abuser attempts to vilify his ex-girlfriend in hopes that, if your paths should ever cross, your paths won't cross. Get my drift? In other words, should she contact you or you meet her by chance, you won't believe whatever crazy talk comes from her mouth. The abuser relies on this. Blaming the ex-partner also serves as a secondary red-flag; no accountability. "It's all her fault" in fact most of what he tells you about his past is always someone else's fault. Let's unpack this, shall we? Here a few scenarios in which an abuser may transfer accountability:

- He failed to accomplish a relatively common milestone such as graduation or obtaining his driver's license. "My mother would not take me to the written exam," or "My English teacher wouldn't give me a passing grade." His failures are everyone else's fault.

- He has children from a previous relationship and does not emotionally or physically support his children (notice I excluded financially). "My child's mother won't let me see my kids," or "I lost visitation because I didn't have an attorney." *Please note this is not legal advice, however most family court systems have several resources for pro se or unrepresented parties and may support the father having visitation. Visitation is difficult to lose, short of the father being a sex offender or illicit drug abuser. In other words, where there is the will to see your children, there is a way to see your children.

- He has outstanding financial obligations. I'm not talking an unpaid parking ticket, but debt that the average person pays because it is required to function as an adult. This includes judgments for unpaid rent, student loan defaults, and vehicle repossession.

Refusing to take responsibility is quite serious. This is also a clinical symptom of anti-social personality disorder also known as sociopathy, just as I mentioned in chapter two.

Perhaps your partner compared you to his ex-lover in the beginning of the relationship often saying, "You are so much better than my ex". This feels good, and it inflates our self-esteem. When the situation becomes abusive, that will quickly turn to devaluing you. You become "just like" the ex, and these comparisons hurt.

Additionally, your partner may use past relationships to justify treating you poorly. "All men cheat. You were late coming home from work, so I know you were with another woman," may be a common phrase that men hear, but with an abuser this phrase is accompanied by intimidating and manipulative behavior such as going through your cell phone contacts, demanding to see or sniff your undergarments, making you account for your time, or checking the mileage in your vehicle. This behavior is unhealthy and toxic. This thought-pattern may then be coupled with pushes, shoves, slaps, and scratches. We live in a culture that turns a blind eye when a woman is physically aggressive with a man. Case in point, I have watched numerous YouTube videos where a woman believes her boyfriend is cheating. Some of the videos are breakup pranks and others are real-life instances, but in almost each scenario, the female slaps, pushes, or scratches the man, and uses force in some way. This is *never* okay. Now imagine the same scenario where the male is the aggressor. We would see the inappropriateness in that situation almost immediately. We would quickly label his behavior as abusive and unacceptable. Regardless of whom the aggressor is, this behavior is always unacceptable. If this is a constant in your relationship, it is time to reconsider things.

Chapter 5

"Men fall in love with her eyes; women fall in love with their ears." – Hart Ramsey, PhD

Falling in Love; the Whirlwind Romance

Have you ever seen someone in love? Everything feels wonderful, looks wonderful, and life is simply all good. There is a reason for this and it's partly scientific. Scientists have concluded that being in love floods our brains and bodies with hormones associated with pleasure, attachment, and obsession. Lucy Brown, neuroscientist, postulates that love can be broken up into three stages: lust, attraction, and attachment. Dopamine is released, causing pleasure in reaction to stimuli such as sexual activity or touch, particularly in men while oxytocin is released in women leading to attachment, and an increase in trust. Seeing someone attractive can activate the same parts of our brains that respond to opioids and painkillers. Being in love signals a drop in the chemical, serotonin, causing the person to hyper-focus on the object of their desire, preventing them from seeing harmful traits early on in a relationship. That is why a person may seem perfect in the beginning. This period can be dangerous when you have become the prey of an abuser.

It is very likely that the abuser has selected you, initially, based on something they have noticed from afar. Perhaps he or she has noticed that, at work, you are a people-pleaser and work to receive praise from others. It could even be that he or she noticed that you are isolated from others or have few friends. You may even seem to have the "perfect life" and are seen as a conquest. These circumstances are attractive to predatory mates. You may ask, "Well Ce, what does this have to do with abuse?" I'll unpack this for you. To start, the abuser has targeted you. For whatever reason, they feel that you will be easy to manipulate. So, what will the abuser do? Everything you desire…in the beginning. Remember, this person's acts are strategic and the time that you spend getting to the know them, they are making mental notes of your weaknesses, childhood traumas, abandonment issues, insecurities, hurts, and fears. This person is not just listening *to* you, they are coming *for* you. So, when you told him that your father abandoned you, he heard, "she needs a protector". When you told him you feel unappreciated at work, he heard, "she desires accolades and applause". When you mentioned that you were independent and a self-sufficient woman, he heard "she needs someone she can depend on and lead her." In essence, he becomes a protector, a cheerleader, and a supporter/provider, or pretty much whatever you have indicated unknowingly, that you need. His responses become all that you desire to hear.

During this time, your potential mate will don a mask that looks just like the person you prayed for, your Mr. or Mrs. Right. This is to gain your trust and acceptance of him as non-threatening. This can cause you to lower your guard. You know, the one you put up the last time you were hurt. They will become everything that your ex-partner was not, plus all the things you currently desire. I urge you to use dating as a time to observe. This is your time to interview, to collect information, so that you can make an informed choice to proceed. When you do not use this time wisely, and all the brain chemistry that we just discussed comes into play, it is like having one foot already in the trap. You have seen him cuss out the waiter, but your love mind says, "well, the waiter was forgetful." You have notice the change in attitude when you were a few minutes late but your love brain says, "well, I don't like it when folks are running late either." Your excuses minimize the dangers of the disguise.

This is the point at which the abuser increases the level of intensity. This is called "love bombing." During this time, your partner may say things like:

"I've never felt like this before."

"You're everything that I've dreamed of."

"I feel so, so connected to you."

"I can't stop thinking about you."

"It hurts to be away from you."

"We're meant to be." or "We're soulmates."

"Without you, there is no me."

"You complete me."

"If you left, I don't know what I would do."

"I want you all to myself."

   Do people in healthy relationships say these things? Yes. However, it is the level of intensity with which it is done that makes this a sign. The abuser may flood your phone with calls and text messages, shower you with gifts, and insist on taking you out and meeting your every need. No one person can meet another's every need. It is humanly impossible. She may plaster your social media account with compliments, flattery, favorite songs, and poems and you may find that you come to rely on this over-communication as a confidence booster. There is a clear methodology to, what may seem to be, madness. When the abuser sees that their target is receptive, the intensity moves into isolation. This requires an entire chapter in itself.

Chapter 6

"If isolation tempers the strong, it is the stumbling-block of the uncertain." Paul Cezanne

<u>Isolation: I Want You All To Myself</u>

If you wanted to dismantle something, truly demolish it, the first thing you would do is to remove its support. The absence of support is essentially isolation. So let's talk about the components of the average person's support system.

Parents. Even as adults, we rely on our parents or those that raised us. They often know us better than we know ourselves. This can be said for godparents, grandparents and close family members.

Friends. Everybody should have at least a handful of friends that love them in spite of themselves. Friends are our go-to people, in times of joy and jubilation as well as trials and difficulties. They offer that mirror we need in times of true or needed reflection.

Hobbies. These are the activities that if we could get paid for them, we would quit our jobs immediately. Hobbies provide us with a creative outlet, stress relief, and a place to decompress from the pressures of life.

Occupation. Your occupation is the role you fill for a company that in turn pays you for your time. This monetary exchange allows you to be financially independent and for some, working a job may even bring joy and fulfillment.

For most, these are the basics of their support system which allows one to function as an independent individual. Independence, however, is a threat to an abuser. This threat must be neutralized in order for their plan to succeed.

So after the charm, flattery, and intensity with which they have courted you has subsided, the abuser might insist on moving in together. I mean, you are probably spending the majority of your waking hours together anyhow, so why not move in together and "save money"? The abuser has just eliminated his partner's first line of defense should he or she want to leave – their own space. Kicking out someone that refuses to leave is not as easy as you think. We will revisit this later in the *Making Your Exit* chapter.

How often would you say that you talk to your parents or that wiser, older family member that seems to be there when you need advice? Weekly, if not daily? This too is a threat to an abuser for two reasons: (1) this individual may notice the signs that your "love brain" won't allow you to see and (2) this person is also a place of refuge should you need to seek a safe haven. The abuser may say, "Honey, you talk to your mom all the time. In fact darling, I don't think she likes me very much. How about we not go over again for dinner (or not invite her over, or not talk on the phone like you do)? Once you decide to reduce the time you invest in that relationship, mother will definitely notice and may even become upset. The abuser has just eliminated another leg of support when things go awry.

And what about those friends? "My love, you're always with them, I don't like to share you and can't stand the thought of being away from you. I need you, and by-the-way, your girlfriend Sheila made a pass at me. I'm not comfortable with her coming over." And just like that, no more friends.

You love to workout at the gym? Me too, but for you and your partner, this too is an issue. Your abuser may frame the gym as a place where you could get hurt, or guys could harass you, and that morning run that you so cherish could be dangerous. The next thing you know you come home to a treadmill in the spare bedroom and set of 5 pound dumbbells on the table.

Although strange, you go along with it because their concerns seem...valid. You continue the relationship and though the frequency of gifts and whirlwind has tapered off, it's still all roses. Maybe he proposes or you become pregnant. Well, he can't have his wife, or mother of his child working. You leave your job. I have had countless women sit across from me, afraid because now that they want to leave, they have no money and no work experience or even years' worth of a gap in work experiences.

Isolation neutralizes the strong and when your strength is tempered, the abuser can overpower you quickly. Thankfully, this can be reversed. You will learn how to rebuild lost strength in later chapters.

Chapter 7

"Suddenly, I'm beginning not to trust my memory at all" -
Paula
Gas Light (1944 film)

Gas Lighting

The human mind is fragile. It is the motherboard, the captain of all our thoughts, feelings, and actions. When influenced, for better or worse, it controls all that we do and all that we become. For this reason, an abuser's goal is to capture the mind of the victim, then everything else will follow.

In the 1944 film *Gaslight*, a young woman, played by Ingrid Bergman, is manipulated by her husband using psychological games and tricks such as the movement and replacement of objects throughout the home and, isolation of the woman, amongst other things, in order to convince her that she is losing her mind. Although fictionally used in the film, this is a common tactic used by abusers.

I once had a client whose husband would hide and replace her medication, keys, and other objects throughout the house. This caused her to second-guess not only her actions, but her thoughts and intentions as well. Was she able to make sound decisions if she couldn't do something as simple as keep up with her medication or car keys? Was she truly "stupid" as her husband often called her? She soon found herself apologizing for everyday mistakes and occurrences. She often felt confused, uncertain, or just plain "crazy." Her abuser had succeeded in psychologically manipulating her, thus causing her to question her own sanity and judgement. He had successfully overwritten her reality and she's started to believe "it's me, not him."

Perhaps you have a valid point of contention to discuss with your partner. You go to them to discuss your feelings, make your point and hope for a resolution, but at the end of the conversation, you are the one apologizing. Sound familiar?

Your partner may even shower you with acts or things you believe *look* like love but in reality he or she is absent emotionally, withholding affection or a true emotional connection. He may even make jokes or say hurtful things in jest and when you make him aware that what he said was hurtful, you are labeled as "being too sensitive."

Moving the Goal Post

The one constant in any sport is that the player knows exactly what he or she is striving for. The target it always the same, the rules never change, and the goal post never moves. This allows for the player to have some level of predictability when considering an opponent's moves. In abusive relationships, the last thing some abusers want is for a victim to predict what is next. To prevent this from happening, some will move the goal post.

I had the pleasure of meeting and hearing the first-hand account of Susan Still's story of abuse and escape as she recalled the ways in which her husband would "change the game." She mentioned, even after she had gotten his wants and requirements down to a science, he would make up new rules or modify existing ones, in essence, moving the goal post and her ability to successfully meet his demands. This action causes a victim to believe that they are the problem, and if they could only fix themselves, the relationship, marriage, or family would be better.

Under these circumstances you'll never be able to do enough to prevent the abuse. If you stay, you will continue to live in a prison. It's time to break out!

Chapter 8

Green Eyes & Eggshells

A tell-tale sign of an abuser is jealousy. Jealousy is being envious of another person's accomplishments, achievements, or possessions in addition to being fiercely protective. We consider someone to be jealous when they are always suspicious of their mate's behaviors or friends. The abuser becomes the proverbial green-eyed monster.

A textbook sign of jealousy is the irrational belief that you are putting others before your mate. Regardless of the context of relationship, whether family member or friend, your mate is constantly and consistently jealous.

"But how can someone be jealous of my family?" you may ask. Quite easily, you see, because at the root of the jealousy are their own insecurities, self-doubts, and irrational thoughts. He may be envious of your relationship with your father because his own father was absent, so all that time you spend with your father is "unnecessary" in the eyes of the abuser. He may even be jealous of your relationship with your children and say things such as, "you don't hug *me* that way, or care for me in that way."

Perhaps you completed a level of education that he or she did not. This is often a point of sensitivity for abusers. He or she as a result may make snide comments and use your accomplishments to belittle you. Does any of the following sound familiar?

"You think you're so damn smart!"

"For someone that has a master's degree, you couldn't do ____ right?"

"I guess you think I'm stupid since you went to school and all I have a GED."

This is quite common and allows an abuser to manipulate you by causing you to question your own ambition and accomplishments. The thoughts that follow are usually along the lines of:

"Maybe I want too much."

"I think I'm better than him, how selfish of me."

Whatever the thought, this may lead you minimizing your accomplishments and your dreams, and even your existence in order to appease your abuser. For the sake of "keeping the peace," you have left behind your very being. No matter how much you shrink yourself, you will never be small enough to make them love you. Simply breathing may be viewed as a threat.

Chapter 9

"The essence of lying is in deception, not in words." - John Ruskin

Deception: Lies, Omissions, & Trickery

At the start of a relationship, one usually attempts to present his or her best self. Ladies, we make sure that every hair is in place, that our legs are shaved; we even hide the ugly sweats and hair rollers. Guys, you know you do the same, keeping your facial hair trimmed, car cleaned, and shirts crisp. We want the person we are interested in to continue being attracted to us as we slowly allow them into the recesses of our lives. This comes with time and a level of comfortability.

For an abuser, that level of comfortability is irrelevant and has no bearing on being honest and forthcoming. Remember, the sociopathic abuser wears a mask and not only deceives you by lying, but with omitting facts and withholding information that can be vital to your safety. He may give you just enough information to satisfy your curiosity. If you will refer to the *Ex Factor* chapter, he may have mentioned he had a previous relationship but fail to mention the details under the guise of protecting his ex. How chivalrous of him. He may allude to a "run-in" with the law, but say it was nothing, or that it was easily resolved, when the complete details might reveal his propensity for future aggression or violence. The abuser may even profess to be honest and upstanding, so that you will not question his integrity regarding such issues.

Holding back is part of the charm that he turns on. It creates and maintains the fantasy that we discussed in the *Whirlwind* chapter. If he fully exposed himself, the fantasy would disintegrate and there would be no pay-off for him.

Sociopathic abusers are sometimes narcissistic. This means that he also has an exaggerated sense of self, a sense of entitlement, and often exploit and takes advantage of others. In addition to believing that laws and rules don't apply to him, he further believes that he is far more important than anyone else.

Perhaps you have caught him in a lie; you have evidence to the contrary, *irrefutable* evidence. It is likely that he will never take responsibility for the lie, admit fault, and may even tell you that you are lucky to be with him, and that he could have anyone that he wants. "If you leave, you'll never be happy without me," is a common response when the victim decides it is time to end the relationship so she doesn't. He has been so intentional at planting seeds of deceit, that she believes she indeed will not be happy without him.

The purpose of the charm, and love bombing in the beginning was to illicit all the information he could to use against her at a later date. I've counseled countless women who say they have revealed their innermost hurts and traumas only to have their secrets thrown in their face later.

The abusive partner thrives on power and control and any opportunity he may have to withhold something, he will. You may have made plans to travel out of town, and are looking forward to it. At the last minute, he refuses to follow-through, for no reason at all, or simply just because he can.

Chapter 10

Pity makes suffering contagious. - Friedrich Nietzsche

Pity Party for One

No one likes a pity party. They are depressing, lonely, and pretty boring. Abusers extend an open invitation to their victims to not only join the pity party, but hang around and make themselves comfortable.

The abuser may appear "vulnerable" and forthcoming, even sincere in sharing his past traumas, failures, hurts, and mistakes. We like this. It makes us feel trustworthy, connected, and close to them. This too is a methodical and calculated tactic. When someone seems genuine or transparent, it draws the listener in and all that is said appears truthful and sincere.

A perfect example of this very thing can be seen in the film, *What's Love Got To Do With It* (1993). The movie chronicles the abusive relationship between Tina and Ike Turner. There is a scene in which a tragedy has occurred and a young Tina comforts Ike while he recounts his father death. Ike, played by actor Laurence

Fishburne, appears vulnerable and tells Tina, played by actress Angela Bassett, that everyone always leaves him – his father, his women, and all the folks he has made famous. Tina, having her own unresolved abandonment issues from childhood, responds "I'll never do what those others did to you." Got her! She just sealed the deal. Each time she is faced with leaving him, she recalls that she cannot because she "knows what it feels like to be abandoned."

Many victims are guilted into staying in an abusive relationship and going along with the desires of the abuser. Even when they are faced with curses, slaps and propositions that would make any outsider cringe, the victim feels an overwhelming sense of pity for and obligation to the abuser. "I don't want to get him in trouble. I just want him to get help and for the abuse to stop," is a common lyric in the song of those being abused. Why wouldn't you want someone who has harmed you to be held responsible? There are many reasons. Reporting could escalate the abuse and the victim fears unthinkable retaliation. In addition, females are socialized to be liked, and if she gets him in trouble, he and his enablers will be mad at her. He and those who support him fail to realize, however, that it was his own actions that landed him in trouble and not his victim reporting it.

Chapter 11

Submission: What Does God Say?

Disclaimer: This is not an attempt to force religious beliefs upon any person that may be reading this book. While I encourage to you read this chapter, if you are uncomfortable with the framing of the subject matter under this heading, proceed now to chapter 12.

For some, submission is important in a relationship while for others, it can be a dirty word. Many abusers use religion and submission as a basis for their actions. If Christian, they may quote Ephesians 5:22 (NIV) which reads "Wives, submit yourselves to your own husbands as you do to the Lord. [23] For the husband is the head of the wife as Christ is the head of the church, his body, of which he is the Savior. [24]Now as the church submits to Christ, so also wives should submit to their husbands in everything." What many fail to realize is that this instruction is followed by a charge for husbands that reads "Husbands love your wives as Christ loved the church."

Submission in the biblical sense means to follow husband's direction, regardless of agreement because you can trust his guidance, his lead. How do you know if he is trust worthy? Scripture tells us: he loves her like

Christ loves the body (church). How does Christ love the church? He loves with gentleness, compassion, kindness, forgiveness, and patience. These are the attributes a husband must exhibit before his wife should submit.

True submission requires two parts for it to be healthy; otherwise it is twisted and toxic. Many victims stay in horrendously abusive relationships because they feel leaving it will disappoint God, and by staying, they are following God and will be blessed. Christ came to give us liberty from bondage, both spiritual and physical, and wants you to have "good success" in all areas of your life. Can you be successful in your thoughts when you are constantly being told that you are ugly, stupid, no good, fat, an idiot, or anything less than what Christ says you are? Absolutely not. Can you have good success as a mother when your spouse demeans, degrades or belittles you in front of your children? No way. That is not the will of God for your life. If you desire faith-based counseling and are in an abusive relationship, please find a licensed therapist, with a program that is biblically-based. I recently had a client who went to couple's counseling (big no-no) with a pastor who "did it on the side" (an even bigger no-no). The client who was the female, was told that the reason her boyfriend isolated her was because "he loved her so much." My heart sank, and alarms went off immediately. The first tenet we learn as therapists is to "do no harm." This is why I stress that not all clergymen are counselors, and not every counselor is well-versed in the nuances of intimate partner violence.

Lastly, an abuser requires that the victim make him, or her, the center of his or her life. He wants her to cater to his every need, work to please him, and put him before all others including her relationship with Christ. The last time I read my bible, I was reminded that act is considered idolatry.

Chapter 12

"Childhood should be carefree, playing in the sun; not living a nightmare in the darkness of the soul." – Dave Pelzer

Abuse, Trauma & Your Children

It is important to remember that abuse, regardless of how it manifests, is traumatic. Psychological trauma is essentially any occurrence that results in severe distress. Some events can be both physically and mentally traumatic, causing injury to the body and inflicting distress onto one's mind or psyche. Trauma is anything that threatens our well-being or that makes us fearful.

Now, imagine being a child and witnessing a parent being abused. This renders the child a secondary victim, not bystander. Some may believe that if he is not hitting the kids, then that person is okay. This is inaccurate and untrue. Children are like sponges, absorbing all that they see, hear, and experience - good or bad. It doesn't matter if they are in another room, or outside, or otherwise occupied in the home at the time of the abuse. Children are perceptive and can often feel or perceive changes in the atmosphere.

During a violent incident children may even attempt to referee or protect a parent being abused. A child may take-on the responsibility of keeping younger children safe during the incident by seeking help or ushering them to a safe place such as a closet or bedroom.

Unlike an adult, children are unable to process and express trauma as we do. Here is a breakdown of how trauma can manifest in children:

Behavioral. After a traumatic experience, children may withdraw from family, friends, or things that were once pleasurable for them. In contrast, they may also act out. A child may regress in behavior that has been mastered; for instance, they may start to wet the bed, even though it has been a while since they last had an accident. Children may act out in school, seek attention, or even attempt to manipulate other children as a result of a traumatic experience.

Emotional. Children do not show depressive symptoms like adults. It instead manifests as irritability or moods swings. They may feel helpless or fear being abandoned. They also tend to believe they are the cause of any problems in the home, including when parents fight. They may show intense anger that seems unmerited or unjustified.

Physically. "My tummy hurts" isn't an uncommon statement from a child. However, chronic aches and pain that cannot be otherwise explained by a pediatrician could be a psychosomatic symptom. As a result, a child may experience short attention span, or even feel nervous or anxious.

Sadly, these are not the only ways a child can be affected as a result of witnessing abuse. There are more. Children will learn one of two roles in life from witnessing abuse in the home. They learn that you can either be a victim or an abuser. They also learn that violence is a means to solve their problems, and that victims are weak and deserve the abuse.

Maybe you think that because you're pregnant, your child is in the clear and the relationship will improve when the baby is born. The birth of a child however will likely intensify any current issues. That beautiful bundle of joy is also a victim, even before a first breath is taken. Studies show that domestic violence negatively affects the mother and infant both during pregnancy and post-partem. Premature labor, low birthweight, behavioral problems, and increase use in pre-natal substance abuse can result. Infants born to battered mothers were found to have heightened startled responses when compared to that of infants born to mothers who had not experienced abuse.

Perhaps you believe, that your child is young - a toddler - and won't remember what is happening now. Not so. While the child may not recall explicit memories of abuse, these memories can be stored in the subconscious, and cause just as much damage. Scientists have found that the parts of the brain responsible for emotional and cognitive functions are severely impaired from complex trauma. This deficit may lead to severe behavioral problems such as ADHD and oppositional defiant disorder, amongst others. Children that witness intimate partner violence may also develop post-traumatic stress syndrome. You are not the only life at stake should you remain in an abusive relationship. Your children deserve a fighting chance in life as well, give it to them.

Chapter 13

Time to Get Real: Your Relationship in Review

"But it's not really *that* bad, is it?" The reason you have selected this book may vary, but one thing remains true; there are some issues in your relationship that require professional scrutiny. It is hard to see the big picture in its entirety when you're in it. In addition to being on the inside, your emotions, mind, spirit, and will may all try to convince you that it is better to stay, or that leaving is too complicated and that you aren't in any danger.

The reality is quite different. The truth says that you were degraded, abused, mistreated, devalued and living below your potential. How do you reconcile two very different stories told by the same person? Stay connected to the reality.

One tool that allows us to be objective, and something that I often use when counseling clients, is a relationship log. This log is completed by only you and requires full honesty. The extent to which you are honest with yourself will directly affect this tool's success. I will walk you through this how it works step-by-step:

1. Take out a sheet of paper or notebook. You will need something that is easily accessible, and private. You can keep notes in your smartphone or tablet as well.

2. Divide the paper into two sections, either by folding down the middle or drawing a line down the center.

3. **The left column**. Here you will record the event. An event is ANY communication, thought, or interaction you have with your partner. If he or she texts, calls, emails, drops by your home or job, or even if you have a memory, thought, or dream about them, record it as an event.

4. **The right column.** On this side, you record the feeling associated with the event or incident. If he texted and you felt happy, write it down. If she slashed your tires and you were pissed, write it down.

5. Keep this running log for a minimum of one week and be **honest** in your writings. It only works, if you work it.

6. Take time alone to review your notes. Is the relationship healthy or toxic? Are you on an emotional roller-coaster? Are you being berated, devalued, or hated? Do you feel good after contact with the person, or worse? Are you where you hoped you be at this time your life? Is this love or complacency?

Again, no one is judging you. The more real you can be with yourself, the better you will be at making an informed decision regarding moving forward.

Chapter 14

Barriers to Leaving

"Why don't you just leave?" is a question that many victims get from family, friends, and those concerned for their safety. To an outsider, it seems quite simple: if you are being mistreated or beaten, you leave. Those in the relationship know, however that it just isn't that easy. There are a number of implications and reasons for why victims stay. Although reasons may vary from person to person, let's examine a few in detail.

Power & Control. Remember, abuse begins in the mind. In other words, if the perpetrator can control his or her victim through psychological manipulation, by learning the victim's weaknesses and unmet needs, everything else will follow and the abuser will soon have total control.

Threats. I once treated a woman for symptoms related to domestic violence whom, from the outside, appeared well-to-do. She had a lucrative job as did her abuser. Her abuser had never laid a hand on her throughout their many years of marriage but had, however, forcefully coerced her into writing a false statement, and later used the false statement to prevent her from leaving him, promising to turn the letter over to her direct supervisor and the federal trade commission if she did. My client was terrified that her husband would make good on his threats, which would not only leave her unemployed, but facing possible criminal charges. Well, he did. Luckily, she cooperated with authorities, had a stellar work history, and was able to continue on with her career, unscathed.

Financial Dependency. I have treated and assisted countless women in the same circumstance; the husband works while she stays home caring for the children and household. While working in the home is admirable and great for children and functionality of the overall household, it can also serve as a snare to leaving an abusive relationship. It can pose several dilemmas:

- The victim will not have access to funds if she leaves the home

- The victim will find becoming employed difficult because of the time spent out of the workforce and working in the home.
- The spouse has promised to take custody of the children if she leaves, because she has no means of providing for them.

Another example of financial dependency includes the abused partner having to account for every dollar he or she makes. For example, the victim works outside the home, but is required to relinquish her entire paycheck to her abuser. I once treated a male victim who, on his payday, was required to cash his check, buy a pack of cigarettes, and then turnover his paystub, and receipts to his wife. If the numbers didn't add up, there would be hell to pay.

The Children. Some victims stay because they have children in common with their abuser. Perhaps she came from a broken home, and believes that her children having two parents, although abusive, is better than them living in a one-parent home. A victim may be fearful of the abuser taking the children, manipulating them, or lying about the true nature of the abuse and make her look bad in the eyes of the children. I have seen women forced by the abuser to sleep in their cars while the husband and children sleep in the home. Even in this extreme case, something made her stay. Her children.

Pressure from Family. We often set unrealistic standards for our children. We want them to be the best at this, or greatest at that, have 2.5 kids, a spouse, a dog, house and be picture-perfect. They can feel this pressure and sometimes, it can cause them to hide the less-than-perfect things going on in their lives. In short, we just don't want to disappoint our parents. We want to prove that we can fix things, or that we can work it out all by ourselves. Some victims decide to stay in an abusive relationship solely because their family will look down upon them for leaving and some have actually been told, "It can't be that bad. Stay. Don't give up." The truth is that your family can either help you pack, or help plan your funeral service. This is your life hanging in the balance and it is your choice that matters, not their opinion.

Fear. I once heard that fear is simply **F**alse **E**vidence **A**ppearing **R**eal. But for an abuse survivor the scars, threats, and remnants of abuse make fear quite real. For anyone attempting to leave, end an abusive relationship or flee to safety, fear is normal. It could be that you fear for your safety and your family members' safety, or simply fear the unknown. Maybe your abuser has some sort of authority in your community, or knows the whereabouts of your loved ones and has threatened to harm them. It's real and it can keep you bound. Fear is not of God and your freedom lies on the other side. You can look at this way: you already know what it is to be treated less than human. Do you know what it is to be free? You may have lived in that relationship for twenty years, but isn't spending the next ten years in freedom worth stepping out into the unknown? I believe so.

Chapter 15

Making Your Exit

I get it, you're scared. This is normal, under the circumstances. You are with someone that programmed you to be fearful, should you even consider leaving the relationship. You may be saying "This is so hard." I know, and that's also normal too. If it were easy to just leave, I would not have written this book. Hard, however, does not mean impossible.

To be very blunt, as I care about your safety, I must warn you that leaving poses the highest threat of lethality in a victim's journey to freedom. There are risks, as well as benefits, and the road ahead has the potential to be both difficult and trying. Again, hard does not mean impossible and there are many options to help you remain safe. While we cannot predict all that will happen, we can be knowledgeable and prepared for the potential challenges you may face.

Once you have made the choice to leave an abusive relationship there are a few things you should expect. Let me provide you with more detail:

He says he wants to talk. That could mean several things. If it were a healthy relationship, this could mean that he wants to have a mutually respectful and mature conversation to discuss your differing points of view. This is *not* what an abuser means. For an abuser, "Baby, I just want to talk," means "I just want to regain control of you." He is attempting to gauge where you are in your thought process, and gather information such as whom have you been talking to, and where you will go next. He is losing control and doesn't like that at all. It also means that he wants to manipulate you, in person. When your abuser is in your presence, he can use body language, gestures, and eye contact to manipulate, intimidate. or lay on the apologies. What makes if challenging is the fact that your feelings for him don't cease because you made the choice to exit.

He becomes all you needed before you leave. Now all the times you wished for help around the house, assistance with the kids, and repairs to the car suddenly become simple tasks he is willing to do. He becomes all that you dreamed of during the abuse. But this is a façade, a mask that he will only wear until you return or reject his efforts to feign "change."

The abuser's tricks at this point are mild yet dangerous. However, the abuser also has the ability to enlist harsh tactics in order to prevent your exit or to render you as helpless as humanly possible. He may start to play "dirty" just to make you miserable. He may:

- Cancel credit, debit, public assistance benefit cards
- Cancel utilities or insurance
- Remove you as an authorized user on bank and other accounts
- Report a vehicle as stolen if in his name
- Refuse to pay support for the children you have in common
- Take back items he purchased for you or the children such as car seat, crib, clothing

Your abuser may reach out to *your* family and friends in search of allies, particularly those with whom you have issues or poor relations. If you and your mom aren't getting along, she may become a perfect ally. This works as a constant connection, or provides a view, into your world without his actual presence. He can then keep tabs on you with ease. He may ask around or scrub social media for any new information or frequent places you are known to visit. There is a word for this behavior, it's called stalking. Stalking is, in fact, **a crime**. It can consist of behaviors I just described or take the form of incessant phone calls and electronic communications, or unsolicited visits to your job or home.

This behavior can be a sign of something more sinister to come. To protect both you and family members you may request the implementation of a restraining order from local authorities.

Retraining Orders. This legally binding order may be provided upon petitioning the courts in your county or city. It prevents your abuser from contacting you, coming within so many feet of your home, work, school, church or other places. It also officially notifies the abuser that you want no further contact with him or her. In most places, the procedure works as follows:

- You are injured, harmed, threatened, or otherwise fear for your safety.

- The person you are fearful of or defendant is a former romantic partner, parent to your child in common, spouse, or current intimate partner.
- Complete a petition for a temporary restraining order. The judge will review and decide whether to grant the petition. If granted the defendant will be served, and you will receive a copy of the order as well. A hearing date will be set whereby you, the defendant, and possibly attorneys or advocates will appear and the judge will hear both sides, then decide whether to grant the protection order for a period of one year or longer, if needed.
- You should keep a copy of the order and temporary order in your car, purse, work, home, and any place you feel necessary so that you can access it easily.
- Some protection orders, may even award temporary child custody to the petitioner/victim.

Custody. If you have a child in common with your abuser, and there is no custody order, neither of you have actual court ordered custody. This means that either of you can take the child across state lines, and the police will not retrieve the child even though the child lives with you, or the other parent, neither parent has actual legal custody. The same is true for a married couple. This is the reason that when a marriage ends, a judge determines who is awarded custody because neither parent inherently has custody. This can be used by the abuser when you decide to leave as another tactic of manipulation. Let me give you a real life example. I once assisted a young mother who walked into my office tearful and upset. She explained that she had a daughter with her ex-boyfriend, whom she had not been with for the past few months. They had agreed that he would care for their daughter while she worked evenings. One night after work, she returned to pick up the child. The father, who lived at his parents' home, came to the door without the child. He was visibly angry and showed my client his cellphone on which he had pictures and messages of, and from, her new relationship interest. Guess what he did then. He refused to return the child, in addition to degrading her by calling her a whore and slut and slammed the door. Upset, she contacted the police, who legally could do nothing. There was no child custody order, even though the child had lived with my client since birth. I advised her to get an attorney and file for custody.

Beating You to the Courthouse. Although it varies across jurisdictions, in my current state of residence, an abuser can file charges against you simply for making threatening statements. The abuser may facilitate the issuing of a frivolous warrant, and with that warrant you may be arrested and have to wait until your court date to prove your innocence.

Here are a few things that you can do when you feel you are able to and willing to leave an abusive partner. The abuse did not occur as a result of happenstance, it was strategic. So it makes sense that your exit should be strategic as well.

Safety. Designate a trustworthy family member or friend, preferably one that your abuser does not know, and ask if you (and your children) can stay. If this is not possible, contact your local battered women's shelter. It should be noted that here are a few shelters for men, but they are far and few between. The Salvation Army is always an option for male victims.

It is important when staying with family members or friends that they understand the seriousness of your circumstances and that word-of-mouth travels fast. They should be sworn to secrecy and not reveal to *anyone* that you are temporarily residing in their home. You should also make them aware that you have no timeframe of how long you will need to remain there, if that is the case. Ask if they require that you pay rent or contribute to their household. Ask if your children are welcome. They may have good intentions in letting you live with them, but these issues can arise later.

Documentation: Document and put in a safe place, all incidents, threats, abuse, injuries. A great method of documentation is filing a police report. This does NOT require that your abuser be arrested or even notified of the reporting. This provides an account of what happened, and can provide you with credibility, should you need to prove a history of abuse. Photographs of injuries as well as documentation of any medical assistance needed as a result of your injuries should be documented as well. For legal purposes, and admissibility, it is better to have an officer or medical professional of your injuries take photographs but if you must, use your video camera to narrate how you received your injuries, and lastly, your camera for photos.

Post Office Box: You will need a safe place to receive mail. It is private, inexpensive and secure.

Safety deposit box: Keep your important documents, i.e. passports, birth certificates, insurance, social security cards and other papers that aren't easily replaceable should they be stolen, discarded or damaged in a safety deposit box if possible.

Contact: This is difficult for many. You have been programmed to stay in constant contact with those you care about but when you decide to leave, it is important to cease all contact with your abuser. Change your e-mail address, block his number or change your phone number (no matter if you've had it for ten years), deactivate social media and refrain from telling others about your daily plans and future intentions.

Security. If you do not have a security system, invest in one. Even an inexpensive one can be helpful. If this isn't possible, your local hardware store or domestic violence center can provide you with a doorstop that comes with an alarm. Door chimes are easy to obtain and a great way to hear comings and goings in your home. Ask a neighbor that you know and trust know to call 911 if they see any suspicious activities at your residence. Changing your locks is another option or even having the existing locks rekeyed.

Remember, your safety and vitality is the key to escaping an abusive relationship and taking back your freedom.

Chapter 16

Healing & Healthy Dating

It takes time to comprehend all that you have experienced. If you are able to recognize your relationship for what it is – abusive, then you are already on the road to healing and recovery.

Trauma fragments the individual causing emotional, psychological, and even physical pain. In order to heal, the psychological and emotional parts of you must be reconciled. Let's discuss some of the feelings you may be experiencing.

Insecure. Regardless of negative or positive, you likely found your relationship or circumstances to be familiar and therefore secure. Leaving this familiarity can be scary and make you feel helpless and hopeless. Moreso than any other feeling, you may feel unsafe.

Guilt. Guilt is the feeling that comes when we believe that we have done something wrong. This is a common response to someone that has left an abusive partner. You may be thinking, "I gave up on her or him," or that *you* were in fact the cause of all the problems in the relationship. Let me remind you that you are leaving for your safety and sanity and the only person responsible for abuse is the abuser.

Anger. With guilt, comes self-blame which can lead to you being angry with yourself. You may begin to notice things that you gave up for your ex, or that how you compromised your morals. You may be angry for staying as long as you did. No matter the cause of the anger, it is important to feel the emotion and consider what secondary emotion is hiding behind it.

Aches & Pains. Our thoughts, emotions and bodies are all connected and in constant communication. Our thoughts become our feelings and our feelings communicate with our bodies. If you find yourself experiencing unexplained headaches, pains, or body soreness, your stress could be the cause.

Grief. You read it correctly. You could be experiencing grief over the loss of your abusive relationship. Just as we mourn someone who has passed away, we mourn other losses in our lives, including the loss of people or things that are toxic to us. Why would you grieve for someone that hurt you? Well, your ex probably wasn't always hurtful or abusive and at some point, you may have even dreamed together, set mutual goals, or fantasized about growing old together. These hopes and dreams die with the loss of the relationship, and grieving that is okay. Give yourself permission. You are not stupid or weird for it, you're simply human.

My aunt once told me that it's okay to cry and be down in a pit, but you cannot stay there. If you need to cry, do it. Just don't spend the rest of your life in that space. Put a limit on it. For instance, if you wake up feeling like crap say to yourself, "today I feel like crap, but I give myself permission to feel this way for (time limit), and after that, I will move on for today." We can't always be strong, and that is perfectly okay. Sometimes we just need to give ourselves permission to just BE.

If you notice that these feelings linger for more than two weeks, or that you experience fatigue or insomnia, loss of interest in things you once found enjoyable, have thoughts of harming yourself or others, or loss of appetite, you should contact your local mental health authority, go to the nearest emergency room, or call your doctor immediately. Professional help is sometimes required, and I strongly recommend it to help you continue to heal. You have a destiny to fulfill!

Healthy Dating

First off, let me say that I advise my clients to go one year without dating or entering a relationship after leaving an abusive one. Predatory people can see your pain and will likely pounce on it. You need time to heal. Survivors of abuse often realize that they no longer know themselves. They gave up their will and desire to appease their abuser and now are left feeling confused and alone. This is a time of rediscovery. A shining example of this is autonomy or being able to make one's own decisions. I once had a client that chose for she and her children to eat lunch on their patio – something her abuser hadn't allowed her to do. This seemingly small decision was tremendously empowering for her.

You have spent your days in that abusive relationship being overly accountable to another person. Jumping into another relationship too soon is likely to attract the same type of potential mate and recreate similar circumstances. If you do choose to date, here are some tips to prevent you from falling into the trap of an abusive relationship again:

- Be mindful of where you meet potential mates. Are you meeting them in passing on the street or in environments where you can observe them repeatedly (i.e. church, work, the gym etc.)? This will give you some insight into how the person interacts with others.
- Make sure your first date is in a public place. Try meeting for coffee. Dinner can be too much pressure, and a movie gives little opportunity for interaction or observation.
- Let them talk. Pay attention to what they share about themselves. Observe how they treat others like the wait staff, or other customers.
- Be late. On your second or third date, be about fifteen minutes late on purpose or cancel at the last minute. It sounds cruel but again, observation is key. Does he or she fly off the handle as a result? Or do they take it in stride?

- Don't be so quick to tell a total stranger your life story, or take him home, or expose her to your family or friends.
- Investigate. Google the individual, check social media pages and check public records in your county.
- Trust your instinct and don't be afraid to cut your losses early. Your well-being is more important than someone else's hurt feelings.

Some of these tips may seem a bit extreme, but, I believe your safety, well-being and sanity are worth it. Don't you?

Chapter 17

Questions & Answers

1. *My friend or family member is being abused. What can I do?*

    I cannot stress enough how important support is to a victim of domestic violence. An abuser's goal is to isolate their victim and to prevent contact with the outside that could interfere with his power and control of the victim. With that said, support may be difficult to offer but being compassionate, offering an ear, or the option of a safe non-judgmental atmosphere can encourage positive change in the life of a victim. Victims often don't confide in anyone, because the first reaction is to "just leave". If they could leave the relationship, they would've left already. On average it takes them seven times to leave and stay gone.

2. *I am not a citizen of the U.S. Can I be deported if I seek help from the police?*

    Federal legislation, specifically The Victims of Trafficking and Violent Protection Act, allows undocumented persons experiencing domestic violence to apply for a U-visa which is set aside for victims of crime and their immediate family members. A condition of this visa is that the victim must be willing to assist law enforcement with prosecuting the criminal.

3. *I heard about protection orders, but how can a piece of paper protect me?*
A protection or restraining order is a piece of paper, however that piece of paper does several things that can work in your favor and protect you and your loved ones. Protection orders are part of a paper trail that can show your abusers history of, and propensity for, abuse and put on record that you are fearful.

4. *Can abuse in a relationship be the fault of both parties?*
The core of intimate partner violence is one's desire to have power and control over the other. There are couples whose arguments lead to two people physically assaulting each other, which is a symptom of two toxic people- with unhealthy interpersonal skills and

behaviors. The difference in this scenario is the absence of power and control. This may be the case if both parties abuse substances or have mental illness. In intimate partner violence, nothing (e.g. substances, mental illness, anger, money) is the cause, only the abuser is responsible.

5. *Will it get better?*
   In short, no, not likely. Abusers don't believe they have a problem. In fact, they believe that you are the problem. "If I could just be this, or do that or change that, it would get better." No it won't. The abuser will continue to move the goal post.

6. *We have children together. They need their father/mother.*
   Children require safety, security, and structure to thrive. Every hit, degrading word and threat against you- is a threat against your precious child's ability to live trauma- free and make healthy attachments in his or her life. They cannot protect themselves; that requires *you*. They're counting on you.

7. *I have found myself in several abusive relationships. What's wrong with me?*
Nothing is *wrong* with you, but if you are noticing that these types of relationships are habitual, you must examine why that is. We subconsciously project our deficits, so if you believe you are worthy of respect or goodness, it will show- predators will sniff it out. Sometimes, people are stuck in a pattern of abuse that began early on in childhood, or unknowingly reenact unhealthy dynamics in current relationships subconsciously hoping to resolve the issue. Counseling is highly recommended for survivors of trauma, as it allows you to identify issues, process, resolve and learn healthy coping skills in safe, non-judgmental environment with an objective, unbiased sounding board.

Chapter 18

National Domestic Violence Statistics
According to the National Coalition Against Domestic Violence, 2016

- On average, nearly 20 people per minute are physically abused by an intimate partner in the United States. During one year, this equates to more than 10 million women and men.
- 1 in 3 women and 1 in 4 men have been victims of [some form of] physical violence by an intimate partner within their lifetime.
- 1 in 5 women and 1 in 7 men have been victims of severe physical violence by an intimate partner in their lifetime.
- 1 in 7 women and 1 in 18 men have been stalked by an intimate partner during their lifetime to the point in which they felt very fearful or believed that they or someone close to them would be harmed or killed.
- On a typical day, there are more than 20,000 phone calls placed to domestic violence hotlines nationwide.
- The presence of a gun in a domestic violence situation increases the risk of homicide by 500%.

- Intimate partner violence accounts for 15% of all violent crime.
- Women between the ages of 18-24 are most commonly abused by an intimate partner.
- 19% of domestic violence involves a weapon.
- Domestic victimization is correlated with a higher rate of depression and suicidal behavior.
- Only 34% of people who are injured by intimate partners receive medical care for their injuries.

National Resources

National Domestic Violence Hotline
1-800-799-SAFE (7233)

Family Justice Centers
Go to www.familyjusticecenter.org to find a center near you.

Meet the Author

Licensed professional counselor, advocate, & speaker, Candyce "Ce" Anderson is dedicated to educating and empowering others. A graduate of Howard University, she holds a master's degree in counseling & psychology from Troy University and is a member of Chi Sigma Iota, the international honor society for professional counselors.

As a child she witnessed incidents of domestic violence and in her adolescent years, dated an abusive boyfriend. As a survivor, and therapist, Ce Anderson educates, informs and empowers others specifically in the areas of domestic violence, sexual assault and self-development from a place of authenticity. She provides speaking engagements and facilitates training, as well as individual counseling and motivational mentoring.

www.thelovetapsbook.com
@ceandersonlive on twitter and instagram

Thank you Jesus Christ for loving me through so that my pain could be repurposed into provision for others. You never left me.

Suggested Reading

- Bancroft, Lundy. *Why Does He Do That?: Inside the Minds of Angry and Controlling Men.* Berkley Books, 2003.

- Bass, E. & Davis, L. *The Courage to Heal. A guide for women survivors of child sexual abuse.* London: Vermillion, 1997.

- Bradshaw, John. *Healing the Shame That Binds You.* Deerfield Beach, Fla: Health Communications, 1988.

- Cloud, Henry, and John S. Townsend. *Boundaries: When to Say Yes, When to Say No to Take Control of Your Life.* Grand Rapids, Mich: Zondervan Pub. House, 1992

- Van, der K. B. A. The Body Keeps the Score: Brain, Mind, and Body in the Healing of Trauma. , 2014

References

Cleckley, Hervey M. *The Mask of Sanity: An Attempt to Clarify Some Issues About the So-Called Psychopathic Personality*. Saint Louis: C.V. Mosby Co, 1964.

"Domestic Violence." U.S. Department of Justice, 2016. <https://www.justice.gov/ovw/domestic-violence>.

"Statistics." National Coalition Against Domestic Violence, 2016. <http://ncadv.org/learn-more/statistics>.

"Victims of Criminal Activity: U Nonimmigrant Status." USCIS. U.S. Department of Homeland Security, 2016. Web. 28 Oct. 2016. https://www.uscis.gov/humanitarian/victims-human-trafficking-other-crimes/victims-criminal-activity-u-nonimmigrant-status/victims-criminal-activity-u-nonimmigrant-status>.

Made in the USA
Coppell, TX
20 February 2024